100
WIFE PRAYERS

A collection of prayers based on common marriage needs

By Mumbi Namusasi

Copyright © 2024 Mercy Mumbi

All rights reserved. No part of this book may be reproduced in any form without permission.

Website: marriagenotebook.com

100 Wife Prayers

To my loving husband, thank you for being the most loving and supportive husband. You inspire me every day. May God continue to bless you.

100 Wife Prayers

Table of content

01 - Protection and Provision
02 - Fulfilling Each Other
03 - Guarding Our Marriage
04 - Building Healthy Habits
05 - Listening and Understanding
06 - Serving Each Other
07 - Quality Time Together
08 - Sharing Our Lives
09 - Enjoying Our Company
10 - Prioritising Each Other
11 - Loyalty and Honesty
12 - Overcoming Challenges
13 - Walking in Godliness
14 - Caring for Myself
15 - Unity in Decisions
16 - Respect and Humility
17 - Open Communication
18 - Remaining Attractive
19 - Good Community
20 - Finances and Provision
21 - Thoughts and Words
22 - Raising Godly Children
23 - Patience and Self-Control
24 - Supportive Wife
25 - Choosing Wise Friends
26 - Love in Marriage
27 - Temptation
28 - Our Children
29 - Affection and Openness
30 - Peaceful Home and Marriage
31 - Choosing Respect
32 - Trusting My Husband
33 - Loving My Husband
34 - Accept Him Unconditionally
35 - Building My Husband's Confidence
36 - Facing Challenges
37 - Husband's Roles
38 - Husband's Fulfillment in Life
39 - Husband's Work
40 - Blessing His Work
41 - Appreciating His Efforts
42 - Husband's Finances
43 - Sexual Intimacy
44 - Mutual Satisfaction in Marriage
45 - Showing Love
46 - Fulfilling My Husband's Needs
47 - Lust and Infidelity
48 - Strength From Temptations
49 - Faithfulness
50 - Supporting Each Other in Trials

100 Wife Prayers

Table of content

51 - Romance
52 - Love
53 - Intentionality
54 - Appreciating My Body
55 - Caring for Myself with Love
56 - Speaking Positively About My Body
57 - Self-Care
58 - Trusting My Husband
59 - My Husband's Love
60 - Trusting God
61 - Accepting Him Without Controlling
62 - His Fulfillment at Work
63 - Financial Stewardship
64 - Protect Our Marriage
65 - Teach Me To Meet His Needs
66 - Overcoming Temptations
67 - My Husband's Trust in God
68 - Fear and Anxiety
69 - Inviting God into My Husband's Work
70 - My Husband's Wisdom
71 - My Husband's Health
72 - Protection Over My Husband
73 - Thank You God
74 - Humility in Success
75 - My Husband's Reputation

76 - My Husband's Godliness
77 - Godly Friendships
78 - His Fatherhood
79 - Keeping Romantic Love Alive
80 - Our Attitude and Words
81 - Overcoming Childhood Trauma
82 - My Attitude Towards Him
83 - My Husband's Struggles
84 - Supporting Him
85 - Appreciating My Contribution
86 - Understanding My Emotions
87 - Giving Him Freedom
88 - My Communication
89 - Acknowledging His Achievements
90 - Repentance and God's Favor
91 - His Christ-like Love
92 - My Husband's Leadership
93 - Make Him Intentional
94 - Love and Faithfulness
95 - His Interest
96 - His Support and Affection
97 - Spiritual and Emotional Support
98 - Relationship with In-laws
99 - My Reputation
100. Devoted to Love

100 Wife Prayers

Introduction

As a young wife, I struggled for a long time to understand what marriage entailed and my role as a wife for a very long time. Most of the things I attempted, based on my limited knowledge, ended up causing more arguments and pain. Then day, I remembered that I had a God who cared for me and wanted to Help me.

I will instruct thee and teach thee in the way which thou shalt go: I will guide thee with mine eye.
Psalm 32:8 KJV

The moment I started praying, I felt like a big piece of luggage had been removed from my shoulder. I didn't have to figure it out on my own anymore. I had a powerful God who could see through the future and knew what was best for me and my husband.

Be careful for nothing; but in every thing by prayer and supplication with thanksgiving let your requests be made known unto God. And the peace of God, which passeth all understanding, shall keep your hearts and minds through Christ Jesus.
Philippians 4:6-7 KJV

My prayer for you is that through this season, you will learn the habit of submitting your marriage and husband to God and trust Him to guide you.

Trust in the LORD with all thine heart; And lean not unto thine own understanding. In all thy ways acknowledge him, And he shall direct thy paths.
Proverbs 3:5-6 KJV

100 Wife Prayers

I encourage you to use these prayers as an inspiration. As you read them, note down anything that stands out and then continue to pray on it. God is able and willing to do what you need if you believe.

Read your Bible and listen to the word of God to encourage your faith. The more you hear about ordinary people like you praying and hearing from God, the more you believe.

Remember the word of God is alive and active. (Read Hebrew 4:12). Build a relationship with God by involving Him in every area of your life.

Commit thy works unto the LORD, And thy thoughts shall be established. Proverbs 16:3 KJV

Join our community on Instagram @marriagenotebook to get daily inspiration as you take this journey.

100 Wife Prayers

A Prayer For You

Heavenly Father, I praise you and honor Your Name. You are faithful and a caring Father, who is ever-present. I pray that you will guide …………………………….. In their marriage. Counsel them, instruct them and teach them in the way they should go. Let the Holy Spirit teach them how to pray for their marriage and intercede on their behalf. Heal every part of their lives that is hurting and restore every part that is broken in Jesus' Name. May they testify of your faithfulness in Jesus' Name, Amen.

100 Wife Prayers

Pray without ceasing
1 Thessalonians 5:17 KJV

01

Protection and Provision

Dear Lord, thank you for protecting and keeping us safe throughout the years. I pray for Your protection of our health, children, marriage, family finances, business, and peace. Please break any strongholds that have held us down this day in Jesus' name. Release us from curses, evil thought patterns, and self-destructive behaviour, and give us a hearts that seeks after Your will in the name of Jesus Christ. I commit all our plans into your hands. Be our shield and our stronghold. In Jesus' Name, Amen!

Reflect on: Psalm 18:2

02

Fulfilling Each Other

Dear Lord, I commit our needs as a couple to your hands. Teach us how to fulfil each other as husband and wife and prevent us from seeking fulfilment outside our marriage. Whenever we feel neglected, please give us the right words to express our needs appropriately. I pray that we both perceive each other's love language and feel content in marriage all our days, in Jesus' Name, Amen!

Reflect on: Mark 10:9

03

Guarding Our Marriage

Father in Heaven, please help us rely on your wisdom and protection all our lives. Remind us to keep healthy boundaries with persons of the opposite sex and break any unhealthy relationships that would destroy our marriage. Help us speak with love and compassion, especially when we are in distress. Give us the words to speak when we need to communicate our needs to one another. Let our marriage glorify You, Lord. In Jesus Name, Amen!

Reflect on: Proverbs 4:23

100 Wife Prayers

04

Building Healthy Habits

Dear Lord, please help my husband and I overcome habits that destroy our marriage. Instead, let us learn healthy habits to build our bond as a couple. Help me fulfill my husband's need for sexual fulfillment and help him meet my need for intimacy and affection. Where either of us lacks interest in the other, please help us develop the attraction. Show us how to win each other's hearts and always look out for each other's interests in Jesus' Name, Amen!

Reflect on: Philippians 2:4

05

Listening and Understanding

Dear Lord, please help my husband and I be quick to listen and slow to speak. Help us understand the extent of each other's needs without judgment or criticism. Replace our resentment toward one another with forgiveness and understanding. Help us look at each other's good side and love one another. I pray that our conversations will be interesting and that we will both have conversation etiquette, giving each other time to speak, listening to each other and using helpful and encouraging words. When we disagree, please help us control our tongues and not use words to hurt each other. Instead, show us how to resolve conflict in a loving way, and seek help where we need it. In Jesus' Name, Amen!

Reflect on: James 1:19

06

Serving Each Other

Thank You, Lord, because we can rely on your wisdom and guidance in our marriage. Thank you for teaching us the importance of meeting each other's needs as a couple. Please help us follow through because sometimes we fail due to a lack of discipline. Protect our marriage from words, thoughts, and actions that would break it. Help us not to do anything out of selfish ambition but to look out for each other's interest in all situations. Give us a heart of service that seeks to make the other feel loved and cared for. Lord, please let our marriage be a source of peace and fulfillment and not a source of anger and resentment all our days. In Jesus' Name, Amen!

Reflect on: Ephesians 6:7

07

Quality Time Together

Dear Lord, please help us create quality time with undivided attention for each other. Give us interest in each other's lives, and let our time together be fun and fulfilling. Show us how to balance work and family life so that we don't neglect each other and give us the grace to enjoy our life together. Help us learn to entrust each other with our plans and issues and how to pray and support each other. I pray that I will be my husband's best friend and he will be my best friend all our days in Jesus' Name, Amen!

Reflect on: Proverbs 5:18

08

Sharing Our Lives

Dear Lord, help my husband and I remain interested in each other's lives. Help us share our intimate lives, know each other inside and outside, and still love each other. Let us share our desires, plans, and struggles freely. Teach us a prayerful habit as a form of supporting each other, forgiveness, and understanding, just as you forgive and understand us. Make us partners with deep respect for one another all our days in Jesus' Name. Amen!

Reflect on: Ecclesiastes 4:9

09

Enjoying Our Company

Dear Lord, thank you for all the wonderful things you have done in my marriage. Today, I commit our recreational activities to Your hands. Help us find mutually fun and engaging activities to do together as a family and as a couple. Help us enjoy each other's company and have fun together. Show me how to surprise my husband with something he will enjoy and show him how to surprise me as well. Grow our romantic love for each other so that even as we grow old together, we still spark each other's hearts. Let us not neglect to date each other and show us creative ways to continue making each other feel special. In Jesus' name, Amen!

Reflect on: Proverbs 5:18

10

Prioritising Each Other

Dear Lord, please make me my husband's favourite person and him mine. Let us enjoy spending time together and build our bond as we do. Help us both prioritize one another in everything and consider each other when making plans. I pray that we will agree on our plans by Your grace and that we will put You first in everything. Show us how to fulfil each other deeply and help us remain desirable to each other only. Let us not entertain any romantic feelings and thoughts with other people outside our marriage. If either of us has a relationship that is a risk to our marriage, I pray that you break it in Jesus' Name. Amen!

Reflect on: Romans 12:10

11

Loyalty and Honesty

Thank you, Lord, for the loyalty and honesty in my marriage. I pray that You continue to help us remain honest and true to each other. Give us self-control and teach us how to resolve issues while looking out for each other. Show us areas in our marriage that pose a risk and give us the heart to work on ourselves. Help us accept each other just the way we are and maintain realistic expectations from each other. I pray that You will be at the centre of our marriage in every way and that our marriage will glorify You, LORD. I submit my marriage into your hands and leave it to you to protect it. Let neither of us be anxious because of our marriage, and instead, help us to always look to You for guidance all our days, in Jesus' Name, Amen!

Reflect on: Proverbs 11:3

12

Overcoming Challenges

My wonderful Father in Heaven, thank you for my marriage. I glorify you, Lord because you have been a present help in my marriage. Time and time again, my husband and I have faced difficulties, but You have helped us overcome them all. I thank You for the wisdom You have given us throughout our relationship and acknowledge that we couldn't have done it without You. Father, You are great and mighty; with you on our side, nothing will be able to defeat us. Please give us a hunger for You, Lord, so that we will have your wisdom and guidance in everything we do. My marriage will thrive by the power of my all mighty God in Jesus' Name, Amen!

Reflect on: Philippians 4:13

13

Walking in Godliness

My excellent and wonderful Father, thank You for changing and renewing our minds. Help us walk in the spirit and not in the flesh. Help us live a Godly life and set the right example for our children. Show us how to build an intimate relationship with You, Lord, so we can have your presence in our marriage all our days. I pray that you teach us to seek first your will and trust in your direction even when it doesn't make sense. Speak to us and help us hear your voice. Teach us the habit of daily prayer and reading the word of God, and help us worship and delight in You all our days; in Jesus' Name, I pray, Amen!

Reflect on: Galatians 5:25

14

Caring for Myself

Heavenly Father, please help me care for myself internally and externally to remain healthy and rejuvenated. Teach my husband how to support me as my body goes through biological and physical changes throughout our lives. Let me stay attractive and fulfilling to him all our days. Help me love, accept, and treat my body respectfully, acknowledging that it is the temple of the Holy Spirit. Give us immense love and acceptance of each other, and let us speak life to each other in Jesus' Name. Amen!

Reflect on: 1 Corinthians 6:19

15

Unity in Decisions

My wonderful Father in Heaven, please help my husband and I agree on our plans and choices. Guide us in every decision, whether big or small and help us consider each other when planning. Let neither of us be selfish, but show us how to agree because you know what's best for us. I pray that our house will be united and You will be at the centre of our lives. Give us wisdom and discernment when making major decisions like where to live, how to raise our children, work, finances, community, and friends. Train us to submit our plans to You, and you will establish them for us. In Jesus' Name, I pray. Amen!

Reflect on: Ecclesiastes 4:12

16

Respect and Humility

Heavenly Father, please help us be honest with one another and hold each other accountable when we make a mistake. I pray that we have unconditional respect for each other and love one another in all circumstances. Where there is pride in our hearts, please exchange it with humility. Let us not treat each other with contempt or think ourselves better than the other. Instead, I pray that we will submit to one another and treat each other respectfully. Wherever there is unforgiveness and resentment in our hearts, please help us forgive, and once we forgive, let us not keep repeating each other's past mistakes to hurt each other. Give us a heart to understand that we make mistakes and love each other despite our weaknesses; in Jesus' Name, Amen!

Reflect on: James 4:10

17

Open Communication

Dear Father in Heaven, please help me be honest with my husband about my struggles, especially when I need his support. Help my husband feel comfortable opening up to me whenever he needs my support. I pray that neither of us judges the other harshly even when our ideals don't align, but instead, we seek to understand where one is coming from. Forgive us for the times we have failed each other, and show us how to be more supportive of each other. Help us respect each other's opinions as they come and give us wisdom to know when and how to offer help where needed. Remind us to cover each other with prayers and encourage and affirm one another, especially when we are going through seasons of transition, difficulties, or growth. Lord, I pray that we will both be each other's peace all our days, in Jesus' Name, Amen!

Reflect on: 1 Thessalonians 5:11

18

Remaining Attractive

Dear Lord, I pray that you help my husband and I remain attractive to one another all our days. Help us submit all our issues to You in faith and have God's peace guard our hearts and minds. Show me what my husband needs from me and make me an expert in fulfilling his marital needs. Show my husband what I need from him and make him an expert in fulfilling my needs. Lord, you know what each of our hearts longs for, even when we have no words to describe our needs. Therefore, I ask that you train me to be the best wife to my husband and train him to be the best husband to me. If we resist your direction in our marriage, please do not be harsh with us, but soften our hearts and make us desire to fulfil our marital obligations. You can change us. Therefore, I ask that You work in our daily habits so that they are pleasing to You, Lord, and beneficial to our marriage. In Jesus' Name, Amen!

Reflect on: Songs of Solomon 1:15

19

Good Community

Dear Lord, I pray that you surround us with a good community. Let us have God-fearing people around us whom we can look up to. Let the people we associate with constantly, at work, in church, or in our neighbourhood, be God-fearing and respectable people who can hold us accountable and mentor us as we mentor them. I pray that we are also good people in the society with respectable reputations. Let us have a support system and a quality social life and live in harmony with other people around us. In Jesus, Name, Amen!

Reflect on: Proverbs 13:20

20

Finances and provision

Our Father in Heaven, thank you for providing all that we need. I pray that you give my husband the ability to consistently provide for us and help us be good stewards of the finances and resources you have given us. Show us where to invest our finances and help us to always honour the Lord with our wealth. Let us meet our financial needs and store up for the future. I pray that You give us contentment with all that You have given us and help us be grateful at all times, submitting our needs to You with complete confidence that You will provide for us. I pray that you bless our work and establish our plans for us, in Jesus' Name, Amen!

Reflect on: Philippians 4:19

21

Thoughts and Words

My wonderful Lord, today I'm grateful for the wisdom that you have given me as a wife and mother and for guiding my husband in his family life. Please help us keep our thoughts pure and help us take every thought captive that is against the knowledge of God. Protect our minds from being overwhelmed by fear and anxiety from the enemy and help us think about honourable and noble things. When we speak, help us speak words that please You with Godly wisdom. Give us wisdom and discernment in everything we do, and help us fear and honour You, our Lord. I commit our minds and thoughts to your hands. In Jesus' Name, I pray, Amen!

Reflect on: Philippians 4:8

22

Raising Godly Children

Dear Lord, I thank you for our children. I pray that you guide us in teaching them diligently in your ways. Give us the wisdom to understand their needs and help us raise them in the way they should go. Help us love them unconditionally and let our children perceive our love. I pray that we live a Godly lifestyle and teach them habits of prayer, Bible study, and building a relationship with You. Provide us with Godly parent mentors with whom we can learn and commune. I commit our children's lives into your hands. In Jesus' Name, I pray. Amen!

Reflect on: Proverbs 22:6

23

Patience and Self-Control

Heavenly Father, I pray that you give my husband and I patience and self-control over our emotions. Help me be my husband's peace and not a quarrelsome wife. Help my husband not treat me harshly but with an understanding of my weakness. Let him love me as Christ loves the church, and let me show him respect and submission as unto the Lord. Help us seek each other's interest even in conflict. Give us self-control when feeling frustrated or disappointed with each other. I pray that we will be slow to speak and slow to become angry and quick to forgive each other in Jesus, Name. Help us also be patient with our children and not exasperate them. I pray that our home will be a home of peace. In Jesus' Name, Amen!

Reflect on: Philippians 4:5

24

Supportive Wife

Dear Lord, please make me a supportive wife to my husband. Help me see his value and genuinely appreciate and affirm him. Show me whenever he is low and needs my encouragement, and give me the right words to build him up. Help me accept him as he is and see his abilities and values. Teach me how to pray for him, and show me the areas I need to cover. I pray that you make me the wife my husband needs in every way. In Jesus' Name. Amen!

Reflect on: Proverbs 31:11

25

Choosing Wise Friends

Father in Heaven, please help my husband and I surround ourselves with true, encouraging friends who mean the best for us. Give us wise, supportive friends who can hold us accountable and encourage us when things get difficult. Replace any friends who plot against us or mean to harm us in any way. Protect our name from destruction by malicious people and give us discernment when choosing friends. Let us also be good friends to other people. I pray to make us hospitable, kind, and generous to our friends and people who need us in Jesus' Name. Amen!

Reflect on: Proverbs 13:20

26

Love in Marriage

My good and wonderful father, I ask that You help my husband and I be irresistible to each other. Help us have a passionate, loving marriage and enjoy it in every way, all our days. Give us your blessing, favour, and protection from all forms of evil. Let our marriage be a source of joy and not sorrow, in Jesus' Name. Amen!

Reflect on: Proverbs 5:19

27

Temptation

Father in Heaven, please eliminate anything or anyone that would bring us to ruin and help us not entertain thoughts or behaviours that would go against our marriage and Godly life. Let our desires be within the marriage boundaries and not sinful. Where we have sinned, I pray that you forgive us and cleanse us from the sin and its consequences. Give us eyes only for each other, and let us be keen to meet each other's matrimonial needs so we don't give the devil room. In Jesus' Name, Amen!

Reflect on: 1 Corinthians 10:13

28

Our Children

My wonderful Father in Heaven, I thank you for our lovely children. Please help us set the right example for them. Let us teach them to be kind, caring, and genuinely loving. Help us do acts of service without selfish ambition so that our children will learn from us. I pray that you protect our children from any form of danger, disease, accident, or injury. Protect them also from any forces of darkness against them and help them learn to submit to you in every way. I pray that our children will love the Lord with all their hearts and will lead a life that pleases You, Lord, in Jesus' Name, Amen.

Reflect on: Psalm 127:3

29

Affection and Openness

Father in Heaven, please help my husband show me affection in a way that will make me feel loved. Help him make time for family and let us have deep, intimate conversations. Help my husband be open and honest with me, provide for our family, and remain a committed family man in Jesus' Name, Amen!

Reflect on: Ephesians 5:25

30

Peaceful Home and Marriage

My wonderful Father in Heaven, please help me meet my husband's needs and fully satisfy him. Help me remain attractive to him and have fun with him all our days. Show me how to create a peaceful and restful home for him and our children. Show us how to navigate our world so that we both serve and support each other. Let us both be irresistible to each other as husband and wife all our days. In Jesus' Name, I pray. Amen!

Reflect on: Proverbs 18:22

31

Choosing Respect

Dear Lord, I pray that you help me to choose to respect my husband in all circumstances. Help me respect him unconditionally, even when I don't feel like it. Show me where I am controlling and help me trust in his judgment. Let me accept him as he is and support who he is without trying to change him. Whenever he is wrong, I pray that you guide him to do the right thing and give me the right words to tell him when I disagree with him. I commit my marriage in your hands; guide my husband and I. In Jesus' Name, I pray. Amen!

Reflect on: Ephesians 5:33

32

Trusting My Husband

Dear Father, please help me trust in my husband's abilities, judgment, and decisions. Let me not second guess or criticize everything he does, but instead, respect his viewpoint. Show me traits in him that will inspire my respect and admiration for him. Whenever I'm in doubt, please give me the right words to express my disagreement without disrespecting or undermining him. When he is wrong, I pray that you make things work for good and help him learn and grow from his mistakes. Guide him, give him wisdom, and straighten his path. In Jesus' Name, Amen!

Reflect on: Ephesians 5:23

33

Loving My Husband

Dear Lord, I pray that you help me love my husband the way that he needs me to. Give me the right words to build him up and encourage him. Let me accept his ideas as they are and affirm him. Please give me self-control with my words so that I never criticize or disrespect him, especially in front of other people. In Jesus' Name, I pray. Amen!

Reflect on: Matthew 6:33

34

Accept Him Unconditionally

Dear Lord, I ask that you help me assume the best about my husband. Let me look at his good side and show him respect and admiration. Let me never bash him in front of others and respect him even in his absence. Show me my husband's admirable qualities and help me compliment him and build him up often. Give me a deep respect for my husband and let him perceive it. In Jesus' Name, I Pray, Amen!

Reflect on: Luke 6:31

35

Building My Husband's Confidence

Dear Lord, please give my husband confidence in his abilities. Remind him that he can do everything through Christ who strengthens him and that he needs to rely on you for direction, not his heart. Remind him of his worth even when he fails so that he keeps pushing. Help me love him with all his faults, and give me understanding so I don't condemn, criticize, or judge him. Let him feel free to open up to me and give me the words to affirm and build up. In Jesus' Name, I pray. Amen!

Reflect on: 2 Timothy 1:7

36

Facing Challenges

My wonderful Father in Heaven, please help my husband take on new challenges with courage and confidence. Remind him that he can do all things through Christ and rely on your guidance. Give him the ability to provide for his family, and bless the work of his hands for him. Let him not run away from responsibilities due to fear, but instead give him courage, strength, and the wisdom he needs to meet his responsibility. Surround him with people who encourage him, build him up, and give him favour in front of God and man. In Jesus' Name, I pray. Amen!

Reflect on: Philipians 4:13

37

Husband's Roles

Heavenly Father, I pray that you guide my husband in his role as husband, father, provider, and leader. Please show him how to fulfil my needs and parent our children how they should grow. Guide him at work, giving him wisdom and favouring working conditions. Help me believe in his abilities and affirm him. In Jesus' name, I pray, Amen!

Reflect on: Colossians 3:23

38

Husband's Fulfilment in life

Dear Lord, please help my husband feel alive and fulfilled in life. Help him feel relaxed and comfortable talking to me about his issues, plans, and dreams. Provide him with supportive friends and mentors whom he can look up to. And remind him to look to you for strength when he feels weary. I want him to feel appreciated at home, show me how to affirm and help him perceive my love and appreciation. Teach me how to help him relax, especially when he is going through a hard time. Protect his mental health and help him seek help whenever he feels overwhelmed. Let me be one of his support systems and his peace. Give us a fulfilling sex life and marriage life so that we are not tempted to seek fulfillment in the wrong places. Let us look up to You for our needs and remember You in everything we do, and You will show us the right way. In Jesus' Name, I pray. Amen!

Reflect on: Ecclesiastes 5:20

39

Husband's work

Dear Lord, thank you for my amazing, hardworking, and efficient husband. I pray that you help him continue to do his best in everything he does as if he is working for the Lord. Bless the work of his hands and help him get paid well. Help him trust in You fully and to never feel overwhelmed by his responsibilities. Supply all his needs according to your riches in glory, in Jesus' Name, Amen!

Reflect on: Colossians 3:23

40

Blessing His Work

My wonderful Father in Heaven. I present my husband's work/business to your able hands. I pray you show him what he needs to do to grow in his work/business. Protect him from any harm at work, whether physical, emotional, or mental. Bless the work of his hands and help him build and sustain wealth successfully. As you bless him, please show him how to help others, help him enjoy it, and have peace. In Jesus' Name, I pray. Amen!

Reflect on: Psalm 90:17

41

Appreciating His Efforts

My wonderful Father, I pray that you help me appreciate my husband's drive to work and help me support him in the way he needs me to. I pray that you help me appreciate his income and use it wisely. Help him enjoy his work and do work that gives him purpose all day. Let him also be content and grateful to You, and keep him from loving and obsessing about money in an unhealthy way. Help him work his best and let him get paid well and even more. Remind him to pray, believe what you say about him, and rely on you with all his heart, in Jesus' Name, Amen!

Reflect on: 1 Thessalonians 5:18

42

Husband's Finances

Father in Heaven, thank you for keeping your promises to my husband and answering his prayers. As you bless him, help him remain humble and respectful and treat others with kindness, giving you all glory. Help him be grateful for what you have given him, and help him remember to tithe and provide for his family and those who may need his support. Show him where to invest his earnings, multiply his earnings, and fill his storehouse till there is no more room. Keep his finances safe from the devourer and let him have peace, knowing that You will never leave him. You are his Father, his provider; I thank You because You have supplied all his needs according to Your riches in glory. In Jesus' Name, Amen!

Reflect on: Deuteronomy 8:18

43

Sexual Intimacy

Father in Heaven, I pray that you help me desire my husband sexually. Help me fulfil his emotional and physical need for sexual fulfilment. When making love, please help me be active and engaged and let me enjoy and feel fulfilled. I pray that our lovemaking will be a source of fulfilment and that our marriage will be strongly bonded. In Jesus' Name, Amen!

Reflect on: Corinthians 7:3

44

Mutual Satisfaction in Marriage

Dear Lord, I realize how emotionally and physically important a mutually fulfilling sexual life is for my husband. I pray that you help us both enjoy it and let it be a source of comfort for both of us. Give my husband the ability to bring me to a satisfying climax and me him. Let us not burn with passion for people outside our marriage but instead be passionate about each other. Help us not to deprive each other of sex so that we are not tempted to sin. Keep us both loyal and let us look to each other for the satisfaction of our physical and emotional sexual needs, in Jesus' Name, Amen!

Reflect on: 1 Corinthians 7:4

45

Showing Love

Dear Lord, please help me show my husband how much I love and adore him in words and actions. Let him perceive my love for him and trust me completely. Help me love him the way that he needs me to, and let me prioritize his needs and fulfil them wholeheartedly. Help me feel confident, loved, and desirable in our marriage. In Jesus' Name, Amen!

Reflect on: 1 John 3:18

46

Fulfilling My Husband's Needs

My wonderful Father, you know my husband's sexual desires; I pray that you show me how to fulfil them. Please help me be attentive and passionate in bed with him. Help me prioritize our sex life and his essential needs. Show me how to communicate my needs as well, and let me trust him to fulfil them. If at all there is sexual trauma in either of us, Father, please heal us and break us from its hold in Jesus, Name. If there are memories from previous relationships in either of our minds, I pray that you help us forget them and focus on each other. I thank you for our strong sexual and emotional bond. In Jesus' Name, Amen!

Reflect on: Proverbs 5:19

47

Lust and Infidelity

My good and faithful Father in Heaven, I come before you to ask that you strengthen my husband so that he doesn't fall into temptations of lust and infidelity. I pray that you help us both avoid situations that would lead us to sin at all costs. Help us control our thoughts so that we only think about good things and are not led to sin by our desires. Let us not entertain any thoughts or feelings of lust and instead channel all our desires within the marriage, in Jesus' Name, Amen!

Reflect on: 1 Corinthians 6:18

48

Strength From Temptations

Father in Heaven, I thank you for being faithful and giving us a way when our desires tempt us. Please help us not fall into temptations. Let us be watchful, pray, and walk by the spirit so that we don't give in to the desires of our flesh. Please also help us lead prayerful lives and lean on you in all our ways. In Jesus' Name, Amen!

Reflect on: Matthew 26:41

49

Faithfulness

Father, Lord, I thank you for my faithful husband. I know that he faces temptations constantly, and I thank you that you give him the discipline and strength to overcome them. I pray that you remind him that he has a spirit of power and self-control and that he can do all things through Christ, who strengthens him. Help him put on God's full armour and have a close and intimate relationship with You. In Jesus' Name, I pray. Amen!

Reflect on: 1 Corinthians 10:13

50

Supporting Each Other in Trials

Thank you, LORD, for your faithfulness in keeping my marriage together. I pray that you help me support my husband the way he needs me to and help my husband support me the way I need. Show me how best to support and encourage him, especially when he is facing trials and temptations. Let me make him comfortable so that he can be vulnerable around me. Give him strong, Godly male advisors and friends to encourage him in his journey. In Jesus' Name. Amen!

Reflect on: Galatians 6:2

51

Romance

Dear Lord, I thank you for the gift of marriage. Help my husband and I meet each other's need for romance the way we both need. Let us gift each other, spend mutually fulfilling intimate time together, hug, talk, play, and enjoy our marriage. Help us desire each other and fulfil each other. Let us not seek marriage fulfilment from other people outside our marriage and show us clearly when we are in situations that can put our relationship at risk. In Jesus' Name, Amen!

Reflect on: Song of Solomon 3:4

52

Love

Thank you, Lord, for my loving husband. Please bless our marriage with love, laughter, peace, and joy. Help us to continue dating and enjoying each other's company. Let us intentionally look for ways to have fun together and make each other feel loved and nurtured. Let us build beautiful memories with each other and look back with peace in our hearts in our golden years. In Jesus' Name, Amen!

Reflect on: Ecclesiastes 9:9

53

Intentionality

Dear Lord, please show us how to keep our love and passion alive in marriage. Let us not use anything as a weapon or form of manipulation for selfish reasons. Instead, help us be intentional in identifying each other's needs and fulfilling them with a cheerful heart. Let us prioritize each other and always do everything for each other. In Jesus' Name, Amen!

Reflect on: Philippians 2:3

54

Appreciating My Body

My wonderful Father, who put me together in my mother's womb, I pray that you help me appreciate my wonderful body. Help me speak on it with love and acceptance. Help me take care of my health and fitness and look after my appearance. Help me overcome self-hate and self-criticism and instead nurture my body. Let me not become complacent and stop taking care of myself. Help me have time, energy, and resources for my self-care. In Jesus' Name, Amen!

Reflect on: Psalm 139:14

55

Caring for Myself with Love

My wonderful LORD, please help me be open and willing to learn how to care for myself. Show me how to care for my health, hygiene, and style. Show me the foods to eat and the best exercises to do. Show me the right clothes, hairstyles/products, makeup, shoes, etc. Help me overcome habits that drain my health and energy. Let me look and feel good, and give me confidence and self-acceptance. I thank you, Lord, for providing me with the resources I need to maintain a healthy, energetic, lively body that I love and appreciate. In Jesus' Name, Amen!

Reflect on: 1 Corinthians 10:31

56

Speaking Positively About My Body

Dear Lord, I pray that you help me stop complaining about my physical appearance and make the changes necessary to be healthy and feel comfortable in my body. Please open my eyes and let me see you the way you see me. Let me love and accept every part of me, and let me appreciate it with my words and actions. Show my husband how to support me in my self-care journey and let him find me attractive in every stage of my life. Help me use positive words whenever I'm referring to my body. Let me also love and encourage other women, in Jesus' Name, Amen!

Reflect on: Proverbs 16:24

57

Self-Care

Dear Lord, I thank you for my supportive husband. I pray that You show him how to support me in my self-care journey. Show him how to love me during the different seasons of my womanhood. Provide him with the resources to help me in my self-care journey and let me be willing to take care of myself. Please encourage me to actively look after myself even when I don't feel like it. Bless my body with youthfulness, and let me enjoy the life you have given me without worrying but submitting my issues to God with thanksgiving, in Jesus' Name, Amen!

Reflect on: 1 Peter 3:5

58

Trusting My Husband

Father Lord, please help me trust my husband fully. Open my eyes, and let me see him as you see him. Let me appreciate him fully and love and respect him completely. Let me accept him as is without trying to change him, and let me learn how to love even his weaknesses. Show me where I have not been understanding and supportive and change my heart toward him. I pray that I do him good always and never harm him, in Jesus' Name, Amen!

Reflect on: 1 Corinthians 13:7

59

My Husband's Love

Father, please fill my husband with love for me. Open his eyes and let him see me the way You see me. Let him appreciate and trust me completely. Let him not do anything to harm me, but instead be good and gentle with me. Let him fulfill me in ways I could never imagine and let me feel safe and comfortable with him. I thank You for giving us this gift of marriage, and I pray that as You use our marriage to bring us close to You, let us also set a good example to our children and those who look up to us, in Jesus' Name, Amen!

Reflect on: Song of Solomon 1:2

60

Trusting God

Thank you, Lord, for being a present help in my time of trouble. I pray that you help me lean on you as my Father. Teach me all the skills that I need in the different roles you have given me. Help me trust in you and remember you in everything I do. Let me practice being grateful, especially with the family you've blessed me with. Let me speak about my husband and children with love, not constant criticism and complaining. Surround me with God-fearing friends who can help me in my journey and show me Godly wife mentors that I can look up to. In Jesus' Name, Amen!

Reflect on: Proverbs 3:5-6

61

Accepting Him Without Controlling

Father in Heaven, please help me accept my husband just the way He is without trying to change or control him. Where I feel self-righteous or better than him, please help me overcome this weakness and see my flaws too. Let me not condemn or judge him but understand his faults as a human being. Let me have the right expectations from him and be grateful for the things that matter. I do not want to be a quarrelsome, nagging, and controlling wife. Please help me overcome these habits and instead give me a gentle spirit. Show me how to support my husband, inspire him, and encourage him. When I need to speak on a difficult subject, give me the right words and let them not fall on deaf ears. Let me not make selfish demands or push my husband away with my critical attitude. Instead, help me to be his peace. I pray that he will always look forward to his wife and be delighted and ravished with my love, in Jesus' Name, Amen!

Reflect on: Romans 15:7

62

His Fulfillment at Work

Heavenly Father, I dedicate my husband's work to your hands. Please help him find fulfilment in working. Help him do what you called him to do. Give him your strength and wisdom, knowledge, and understanding. Encourage him when he grows weary and remind him to rest. Show me how to support him, encourage him, and be his peace. In Jesus' Name, Amen!

Reflect on: Colossians 3:23

63

Financial Stewardship

Dear Lord, I thank you for our ability to earn and meet our financial needs. Thank you because we can pay our bills, support others, and have more than enough. I dedicate all that we earn to you. Bless it and make it more than enough. Help us use our money according to Your will and protect us from loving or obsessing about money in an unhealthy way. Help us put You first with our finances and trust You as our provider. I thank You because You will never leave us. In Jesus' Name, Amen!

Reflect on: Proverbs 3:9

64

Protect Our Marriage

Dear Lord, I thank you for the gift of sex in my marriage. Thank you for helping my husband and I meet each other's needs and fulfil one another. I pray that you protect and strengthen us so we don't fall into temptations. Heal us from any strongholds from the past and let us overcome any memories from previous relationships. Protect our minds and hearts from lasting for other people outside our marriage. In Jesus' Name, Amen!

Reflect on: 1 Corinthians 6:18

65

Teach Me To Meet His Needs

My Father in Heaven, I realize that my husband has needs I am uncomfortable fulfilling. I pray that you teach me and help me be willing to fulfil them. Make me the best at fulfilling my husband's needs. Teach me how to be my husband's best lover, friend, and partner. Show me how to love my husband in a way he understands. In Jesus' Name, Amen!

Reflect on: 1Corinthians 7:3

66

Overcoming Temptations

Dear Lord, I bring every temptation my husband struggles with into your hands. Protect us from being driven away from You by following our flesh. Protect us from adultery, alcoholism, addiction, irresponsibility, laziness, procrastination, lies, lust, and fear among others. Help us bring captive every thought that raises itself against the knowledge of God. I submit mine and my husband's life into your hands. In Jesus' Name, Amen!

Reflect on: Romans 8:13

67

My Husband's Trust in God

Thank You, Lord, for turning my husband's heart toward You. Thank You because he walks by faith and not by sight. Thank you for teaching him to count on You in everything he does. I pray that you protect his mind from being overtaken by lies from the evil one. Remind him that his help comes from the Lord. Fight for him, and he will need only be still. In Jesus' Name, Amen!

Reflect on: Matthew 6:33

68

Fear and Anxiety

Dear Lord, I commit any fear that my husband and I have to your hands. Help us overcome anxiety and paralyzing fear that prevents us from moving forward. Let us remember that we can do all things through Christ who lives in us. Help us have faith in You so that we can do anything in Jesus' name. Teach us to walk by the spirit and remember that You have given us a spirit of power and a sound mind. In Jesus' Name, Amen!

Reflect on: 1 Peter 5:7

69

Inviting God into My Husband's Work

My good and wonderful Father, I thank You for the opportunity to pray and submit all my needs to You. Today, I invite You to my husband's work. Please help him do the work that You will for him. Give him wisdom and direction at work and help him work as though he is working for the Lord. Protect his mind from fear and give him courage to face all things, knowing that he has Christ within him. In Jesus' Name, Amen!

Reflect on: Proverbs 16:3

70

My Husband's Wisdom

Heavenly Father, please make my husband wise. Give him Godly wisdom and discernment. Let him fear and revere You. Guide him when making decisions so that he makes the right choices. Give him Godly and wise friends and self-control over his emotions, especially when making decisions. Let him have wise, Godly advisors at work and in life, and let him not keep the company of the ungodly. In Jesus Name, Amen!

Reflect on: James 1:5

71

My Husband's Health

Dear Lord, thank you for sustaining my husband's health and providing him with the necessary resources to lead a healthy lifestyle. Help him eat healthy, nutritious meals and exercise regularly. Let him not worry about things but submit his issues to God in prayer and thanksgiving. Give him a healthy balance of work, family, and personal time, and let him prioritize a relationship with you, God. In Jesus' Name, Amen!

Reflect on: 3 John 1:2

72

Protection Over My Husband

Thank You, Lord, for giving your angels charge over my husband. Thank you for being his light and salvation. Let him not be afraid, for you are his refuge and safety. Protect him from all the forces of darkness, from rulers of darkness in the heavenly spaces, lies, and strongholds of darkness. Protect him from disease, discouragement, accidents, and any form of violence forged against him. In Jesus' Name, Amen!

Reflect on: Psalm 121:7

73

Thank you God

Thank you, Lord, for teaching my husband how to pray and build a relationship with You. Thank you for renewing his mind and cleansing his heart. Thank you for healing our marriage from all the difficult seasons we have faced. I pray that the Holy Spirit continues to empower us, build and increase our faith, and teach us to rely on God in all circumstances. In Jesus' Name, Amen!

Reflect on: Philippians 2:13

74

Humility in Success

Thank you, Lord, for giving my husband success. Thank you for blessing his endeavours and protecting him from all forms of evil and danger. I pray that you give him humility and a sense of responsibility. As You lift him up, let him not forget the Lord who gave him the ability to succeed. Let him be kind, respectful, and helpful to other people. Help him to take care of his family and never forget his responsibilities. Help him support those who need him, and my Lord, let him remember You and put You first with his earnings. In Jesus' Name, Amen!

Reflect on: Ecclesiastes 5:19

75

My Husband's Reputation

Heavenly Father, I submit my husband's name and reputation to Your hands. Protect him from idle gossipers who seek to destroy and defame him. Shut those who would slander him and defend him in rooms where people plot and plan against him. Let him also walk in spirit and obey You and live a blameless life.
Let him not covet what belongs to another, steal, kill, assault, or destroy any person's life. Keep the enemy away from his ears and give him a strong desire to obey You, Lord. Protect and defend and fight for him; he will need only be still. In Jesus' Name, Amen!

Reflect on: 1 Peter 2:12

76

My Husband's Godliness

Lord, I pray that You help my husband put You first above everything else. Let him seek Your will and fully commit his life to You. Help him pray on every occasion, worship You, and give You all the glory. Make him a leader and the priest in our home. Let him lead by example, and I pray that He pleases You, Lord. Give him counsel and keep Him under Your wing. In Jesus' Name, Amen!

Reflect on: Matthew 6:33

77

Goldy Friendships

I praise You, Lord because I have seen your glory, favor, and power in my marriage. Thank You for teaching us how to be husband and wife and correcting us when we are wrong. I pray that You give us married Godly Christian friends to commune with and a strong Christian community to support each other. I also pray that you make us good and supportive friends in Jesus' Name. In Jesus' Name, Amen!

Reflect on: Proverbs 27:17

78

His Fatherhood

Heavenly Father, I pray that you lead my husband in his fatherhood journey. Show him how to love and support his children's needs as a Godly Father. Let him raise them diligently in the way they should go, and let him bless his children. Let him lead his children by example and leave them a good inheritance. I pray that you help him as His Father in heaven so that he doesn't grow weary. In Jesus' Name, Amen!

Reflect on: Ephesians 6:4

79

Keeping Romantic Love Alive

Thank you, Lord, for my husband's love for me. I pray that you show him how to love me and fulfil my needs. Fill him with compassion and romantic love towards me, and let me perceive his effort. I pray that you help us keep our romantic love and passion alive and help us continue dating each other. Let us treat each other with care and compassion and quickly forgive each other. Let us be patient and understanding of each other's faults and not give up on each other but instead pray. I thank You, Lord, for modelling what love is; help us unconditionally love and respect one another. In Jesus' Name, Amen!

Reflect on: Proverbs 3:3

80

Our attitude and word's

Father in heaven, please help us have the right attitude toward each other. Let us control our words and emotions and use kind and healing words even when we are angry. Let us not hurt each other deliberately or undermine each other. Let us encourage one another and protect each other's feelings. Please forgive us for our failed times and help us forgive each other. In Jesus' Name, Amen!

Reflect on: Proverbs 15:4

81

Overcoming childhood trauma

Father, I pray that you help us both overcome childhood effects and trauma that are working against our marriages. Heal us from all forms of chaos in our hearts and help us get help where we need it. Help us not repeat the mistakes we saw growing up and emulate the right example to our children, in Jesus' Name, Amen!

Reflect on: Psalm 147:3

82

My attitude towards him

Father in Heaven, please help me accept my husband just as he is without trying to change or control him. Let me not condemn or judge him but understand his faults as a human being. Let me have the right expectations and be grateful for the things that matter. I do not want to be a quarrelsome, nagging, or controlling wife; please help me overcome these habits and give me a gentle spirit. Show me how to support, inspire, and encourage my husband. I pray he will always look forward to his wife and be delighted and ravished with my love in Jesus' Name, Amen!

Reflect on: Romans 15:7

83

My Husband's Struggles

Thank you, wonderful Father, for my loving husband. I commit his struggles to your mighty hands, guide him, and strengthen him when he faces obstacles. Quiet his mind from lies from the enemy and help him have thoughts of good report. Let him not think of evil or plan to sin. I pray that You give Your angels charge over him and fill his heart and mind with peace in Jesus' Name, Amen!

Reflect on: Isaiah 40:31

84

Supporting Him

Dear Lord, show me how to trust my husband. Give me confidence in him and help me encourage him when the situation gets tough. Teach me how to pray for and support him, especially when he is going through difficulties. I pray that he will always feel that he can count on me and that I will always be receptive to him when he needs me. Show me where I resist or refuse to support him, and help me overcome the resistance in Jesus' Name, Amen!

Reflect on: Galatians 6:2

85

Appreciating My Contribution

Dear lord, please help me appreciate my contribution to our marriage. Let me see my effort and speak to myself with love. Let my husband enjoy me, too. Help me overcome self-doubt and believe that I am a capable wife and enough. Make me a noble wife according to Your word, and give me a cheerful heart when fulfilling my wifehood and motherhood duties in Jesus' Name!

Reflect on: Proverbs 31:17

86

Understanding My Emotions

Dear Lord, please give my husband an understanding of my emotions and their complexities. Give me self-control and help me regulate my mood changes especially due to hormonal imbalance. Help my husband understand me and accept me the way I am and show him how to meet my needs. Give me the right expectations towards my husband and help me express my needs in a way that he understands. Help him support me emotionally when I need his help and show him my perceptive in Jesus' Name, Amen!

Reflect on: 1 Peter 3:7

87

Giving Him Freedom

Dear Lord, please help me give my husband his freedom and space. Let me not be controlling and selfish without considering his need for independence. Show me when and how to communicate my needs and let me understand his as well. I pray that he doesn't see me as a nuisance but as a source of peace and comfort. In Jesus' Name, Amen!

Reflect on: Prov 21:19

88

My communication

Father, please teach me how to listen more and express myself when communicating with my husband. Help me be interesting and intriguing to him and let him enjoy our conversations. Show him also how to listen keenly and be interested and help him meet my need for intimate conversations. I pray that we don't lose our interest in each other and in fact be more interesting to each other as we grow older together. In Jesus' Name, Amen!

Reflect on: Colossians 4:6

89

Acknowledging His Achievements

Dear Lord, please help me recognize my husband's effort and accomplishment and let me acknowledge it. Show me when he needs my affirmation and admiration the most, and give me the words to encourage him. I pray that you work on his thoughts as well so that he doesn't have limiting beliefs and feels accomplished in his life. In Jesus' Name, Amen!

Reflect on: 1 Thessalonians 5:11

90

Repentance and God's favour

My wonderful Father, I realize that my husband and I have continued to sin and failed to obey You in the past. Please forgive us and help us overcome sin and walk in the spirit and not in the flesh. I commit our future to your able hands. Please establish all our plans for us. Give us success and favour, and let us prosper in the land that you have given us. I pray that my husband and I will enjoy our life together, live in harmony, and leave a good legacy in Jesus' Name, Amen!

Reflect on: 1 John 1:9

91

His Christ-like love

Father in Heaven, please help my husband love me unconditionally. Let him love me as Christ loves the church. Help him prioritize me as his wife and value me in his life. I pray that He will rejoice in me and feel fulfilled in our marriage. Show him how to be my husband and let him meet my needs with a cheerful heart. In Jesus Name, Amen!

Reflect on: Ephesians 5:25

92

My Husband's Leadership

Dear Lord, please make my husband the priest and leader of our family. Let him look to you for guidance to lead his family to Christ. Give him humility and let him know that he has Christ within and doesn't have to rely on his own strength. I pray that You will give him Wisdom in every decision he makes, help him revere God, and help him put You first in everything in Jesus' Name. Amen!

Reflect on: 1 Corinthians 11:3

93

Make Him Intentional

Dear Lord, please help my husband intentionally love me, his wife. Let him make a deliberate effort to meet my physical and emotional needs. When he doesn't know what to do, please drive him to pray and seek your guidance. Give him the right source of information and surround him with Godly mentors and friends. Guide him and counsel him in the way he should go. In Jesus' Name, Amen!

Reflect on: 1 Peter 4:8

94

Love and Faithfulness

Dear Lord, please help my husband love me consistently. Let him spend quality time with his family and demonstrate romantic love for me in everyday life. When faced with temptation, I pray that my husband will choose to honor God and remain faithful to his wife. Fill my husband with romantic love for me and fill my heart with deep respect and admiration for him, in Jesus' Name, Amen.

Reflect on: Proverbs 3:3

95

His Interest

Father in Heaven, please give my husband a genuine interest in me. Let him want to know all about me and find me intriguing and not dull. Give him curiosity and show him how to keep the interest alive. Let him spend time with me, talking and learning about each other. Give him an understanding of my needs and who I am as a person, and let him be gentle in how he treats me. I pray that he intentionally looks for ways to love me romantically and let me perceive his love and feel fulfilled, in Jesus' Name, Amen.

Reflect on: Proverbs 5:18

96

His Support and Affection

Dear Lord, please show my husband how to nurture and support me as his wife. Let him cherish his wife and treat me with tenderness and affection. Show him how to love me throughout the day, every day, and let me accept and appreciate his show of love. Help him meet my physical needs as his wife, and let me meet his. I pray that he encourages and affirms me in life and lets me feel loved and cared for in Jesus' Name. Amen.

Reflect on: 1 Corinthians 13:4-5

97

Spiritual and Emotional support

Dear Lord, I pray that you help my husband be emotionally supportive and protective of me. Let him use loving and kind words. Words that build and not destroy. Let him not use hurtful words in anger and instead give him patience and self-control. Help him support me in prayer and in fighting spiritual battles. Let us pray together, study the word of God together and have a strong spiritual bond. Show him how to be the priest in our family. In Jesus' Name, Amen.

Reflect on: Romans 12:10

98

Relationship with In-laws

Dear Lord, please help me have a good relationship with my in-laws. Help me honour my father and mother-in-law. Help me appreciate and accept them as they are. Where there is a problem between us, I pray that you intervene and let us have peace and come to an agreement. Help my in-laws also love and accept me as part of the family. Show me where I need to forgive my father and let me honour them as well. In Jesus Name, Amen!

Reflect on: Exodus 20:12

99

My Reputation

Dear Lord, please protect my reputation from the enemy. Guide me to walk in your ways and guard my heart and mind, so that I don't speak words that are unpleasant to you Lord. Show me how to live respectfully and peacefully with others, especially with my family. I pray that my husband will respect me and protect me emotionally, physically and spiritually by your grace. Give me mentors to learn from and let me live a life that pleases you, God.

Reflect on: Proverbs 22:1

100

Devoted to Love

Dear Lord, please help my husband to regularly reassure me. Show him how to verbally express his love for me and show it with actions. Help him be affectionate with me and understand my preferences as they are. Show me how to love my husband in his own love language and let us both feel loved and appreciated in our marriage. Protect our marriage and guide us in all our days. Give us the blessing of the Lord and let us enjoy our marriage and our life together, in Jesus, Name, Amen

Reflect on: Romans 12:10

100 Wife Prayers

Thank you for taking the time to pray over your marriage and husband. I pray that the Lord will continue to do what He has started. May He transform lives and restore the years the locusts have stolen.

If you loved this book, we also have a prayer journal with guided prayer prompts to help you continue the habit of consistent prayer. Visit marriagenotebook.com to learn more.

Printed in Great Britain
by Amazon